For ages I kept these tiny slips,
Though why, I never knew
But now I see, through all the years
I Saved This Fortune For You

One Must Dare To Be Himself
However Frightening Or Strange
That Self May Prove To Be

Adversity Is The Parent Of Virtue

A Good Beginning Is Half The Task

Today's A Day To Nourish
Yourself.
Feed Yourself Well.

Curiosity Kills Boredom.
Nothing Kills Curiosity.

Avoid Compulsively Making Things Worse

Never Be Less Than Your Dreams

Don’t Wait For Your Ship To Come In.
Swim Out To It.

Do The Thing You Fear And The Death Of Fear Is Certain

A Problem Clearly Stated Is A Problem Half Solved

Don't Pursue Happiness - Create It

If We Are To Have Magical Bodies, We Must Have Magical Minds

From Error To Error, One Discovers The Entire Truth

Follow The Middle Path.
Neither Extreme Will Make You Happy.

Only One Who Attempts The Absurd Can Achieve The Impossible

The Future Is A Blank Canvas; Paint It As You Wish

Listening, Not Imitation, May Be The Sincerest Form Of Flattery

Never Bring Unhappy Feelings Into Your Home

You Don’t Need Strength To Let Go Of Something. What You Really Need Is Understanding.

Failure Is The Only Opportunity To Begin More Intelligently

The Secret That Leads To Many Goals Is Tenacity

Education Is Not Filling A Bucket But Lighting A Fire

Half Of Being Smart Is Knowing What You Are Dumb About

Good Books Are Friends Who Are Always Ready To Talk To Us

Experience Is The Name Everyone Gives To Their Mistakes

All The Darkness In The World Cannot Put Out A Single Candle

The Ultimate Test Of A Relationship Is To Disagree But To Hold Hands

To Be Joyful Is To Dance In The Rain Of Life

Fresh Ideas Are Not Always The Best Ideas

You Can Be A Victor Without Having Victims

When Spider Webs Unite, They Can Tie Up A Lion

Life Is About Making Some Things Happen,
Not Waiting For Something To Happen

When There Is An Open Mind, There Will Always Be A Frontier

Have A Vision. Be Demanding.

Faith is Personal, But Never Private

Your Future Will Look Like A Grand Adventure

月光局

Ignorance On Fire Is Better Than Knowledge On Ice

Behavior Is A Mirror In Which Everyone
Shows Their Own Image

The Greatest Remedy For Anger Is Delay

Do Not Spend The Money That You Don't Have

Just Because You Put Tap Shoes On An Elephant Does Not Mean It Can Dance

Grand Adventures Await Those Who Are Willing To Turn The Corner

In The Province Of The Mind, What One Believes To Be True Either Is True Or Becomes True

A Good Laugh And A Good Cry Both Cleanse The Mind

Blessed Is He Who Makes His Companions Laugh

Haste Does Not Bring Success

Never Argue With A Fool

Nothing Is A Waste Of Time If You Learn Something From It

The Glass Is Not Half-Empty, It's Just Twice Too Big

The Fortune You Seek Is In Another Cookie

Made in the USA
Columbia, SC
07 July 2025

60477391R00057